My
Creations

Origami Jewelry

Mayumi Jezewski

Dover Publications, Inc.
Mineola, New York

The publisher wishes to acknowledge
Marc Kirschenbaum for his technical edits,
but especially for the origami instructions and
diagrams for the Iris project on pages 18–23.

Bibliographical Note

Origami Jewelry, first published by Dover
Publications, Inc., in 2016, is a new English translation
of *Bijoux en origami*, originally published by Fleurus
Editions, Paris, in 2015.

Library of Congress Cataloging-in-Publication Data

Names: Jezewski, Mayumi, author.
Title: Origami jewelry / Mayumi Jezewski.
Other titles: Bijoux en origami. English
Description: Mineola, New York : Dover Publications,
    2016. | "English translation of Bijoux en origami,
    originally published by Fleurus Editions, Paris, France,
    in 2015."
Identifiers: LCCN 2016010550| ISBN 9780486805641 |
    ISBN 0486805646
Subjects: LCSH: Jewelry making—Juvenile literature. |
    Origami— Juvenile fiction. | Handicraft—Juvenile
    fiction.
Classification: LCC TT212 .J4913 2016 |
    DDC 745.594/2—dc23 LC record available at
    https://lccn.loc.gov/2016010550

Manufactured in the United States by RR Donnelley
80564601   2016
www.doverpublications.com

Contents

Materials

❶ Origami paper
Very thin and easy to fold, plain or patterned, origami paper is ideal to create small-sized jewelry.

❷ Jewelry pliers
They allow you to open and close jump rings, to install ribbon clamps, cord clamps, and crimp beads.

❸ Jewelry glue
This is a special glue that secures your origami piece on any metallic support.

❹ Nylon thread
As it is almost invisible, nylon thread discreetly joins elements together.

❺ Needle
It is useful to pierce your pieces in order to introduce a screw eye pin or a thread.

❻ Earring hooks or posts
An earring hook or earring post (with stud or flat pad) will allow you to add a chain or a hoop to your models.

❼ Finger rings with pads
The flat pad offers a wonderful surface to glue an origami piece.

❽ Brooches
A brooch bar pin includes a pad on which you can glue your origami jewel. The loops of a brooch pin are perfect to attach dangling pieces.

❾ Bobby pins with pads
You can create a hair accessory by gluing your model onto the pad of a bobby pin.

❿ Jump rings
These come in a variety of sizes and can be used to link several elements.

⓫ Screw eye pins
A screw eye pin is used to attach a chain, cord, thread, or link.

⓬ Clasps
Added by using a jump ring, the clasp is usually the final piece to your jewelry.

⓭ Crimp pearls
A crimp pearl allows you to clamp two threads together or to secure your folded creation.

⓮ Chains
A chain comes in handy to hang your creation on an earring post or a brooch bar pin, or to join two elements together. It can also be the basis for a bracelet.

⓯ Ribbon or cord clamps
A ribbon or cord clamp is installed at the end of a ribbon or cord to add a clasp to a jewelry piece.

⓰ Ribbons

⓱ Cords

Add round pearls or sequins as finishing touches to your creations.

You can use varnish or vinyl glue to finish your models. Be careful not to use too much, or your piece will lose its shape.

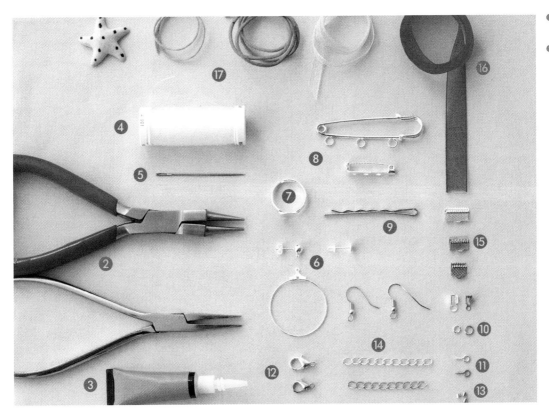

Mounting Techniques

Piercing the origami

Use a needle to pierce your model, being careful not to puncture too close to the edge. For the stars, the needle enters between two branches and comes out at the tip of the opposite branch. That hole can also be used to insert a thread, a jump ring, or a screw eye pin.

Opening or closing a ring

Use two jewelry pliers to pull the ends of a ring in opposite directions. You can close the ring by applying the pliers in the opposite direction. Be careful not to bend the ring to the right or left, which would weaken or damage it!

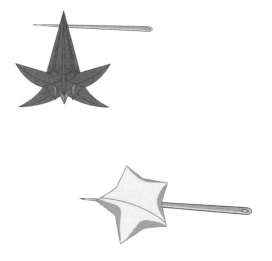

Installing a clasp

Open the jump ring, introduce the last link of the chain and the clasp loop, then close the jump ring, always using two jewelry pliers.

Installing a screw eye pin

Pierce your creation with a needle, and install the screw eye pin in the hole.

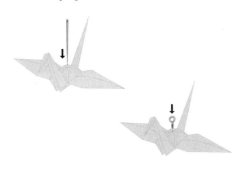

Finishing a brooch, a ring, a hair accessory, or an earring post

Apply a few drops of glue to the metallic pad. Then place the origami piece and apply some pressure for a few seconds. Leave it to dry.

Installing a crimp bead

Thread a crimp bead and push it to the desired spot. Using jewelry pliers, crimp the bead on the thread to set it. After piercing your origami piece, thread another crimp bead and push it as close to the piece as possible so it will not move. Finally, crimp the bead with jewelry pliers.

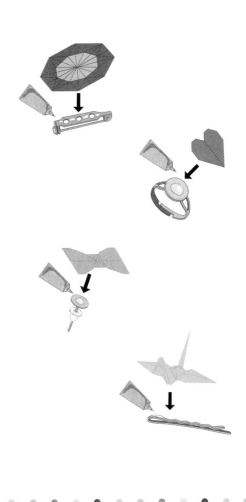

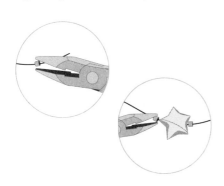

Finishing an earring

With nylon thread and a crimp bead
Thread a crimp bead onto the nylon thread. Insert the nylon thread into the loop of the earring and insert the thread back into the crimp bead. Adjust to the desired length, and crimp the bead with jewelry pliers.

With a chain
Open the first link of the chain, introduce it into the earring loop and close it. You can also join the chain to the earring with a jump ring.

With a jump ring
Open the jump ring with two jewelry pliers. Slide it onto a screw eye pin loop already attached to your model (or directly into a hole punched in it) and attach to the earring loop.

Finishing a hoop

❶ Attach the hoop to the earring post loop with a jump ring. Next, thread the nylon thread through a crimp bead, push the thread into the loop of the hoop, and push the thread back into the crimp bead. Then, adjust to the desired length and crimp the crimp bead with jewelry pliers.

❷ Thread the origami piece and a second crimp bead onto the nylon thread. Next, loop the nylon thread around the lower part of the hoop and insert it back into the crimp bead. Then, adjust the length, and crimp the bead with jewelry pliers. You can cut the extra thread if necessary.

Installing a ribbon clamp

Position the ribbon inside the ribbon clamp, and crimp it with jewelry pliers. Finish it by installing a jump ring on the ribbon clamp loop and attaching a clasp to it.

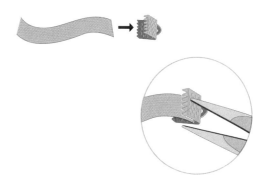

Installing a cord clamp

Position the cord inside the cord clamp before crimping it with jewelry pliers. Finish by installing a jump ring in the cord clamp loop and attaching a clasp to it.

Key to Origami Terms

Note: In this book, centimeters (cm) have been rounded to the nearest quarter-inch (")

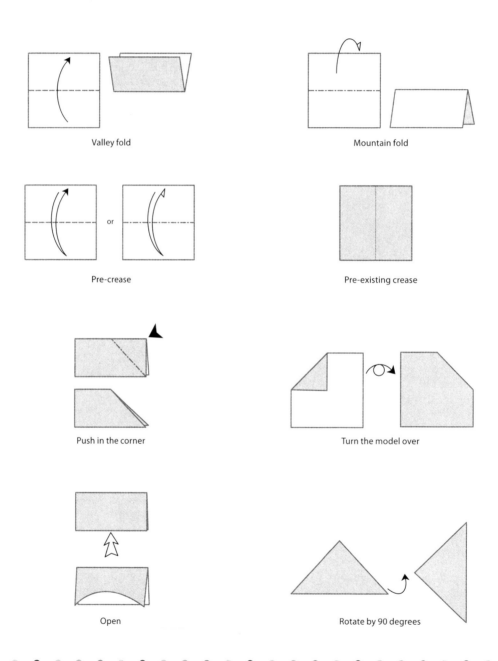

Valley fold

Mountain fold

Pre-crease

Pre-existing crease

Push in the corner

Turn the model over

Open

Rotate by 90 degrees

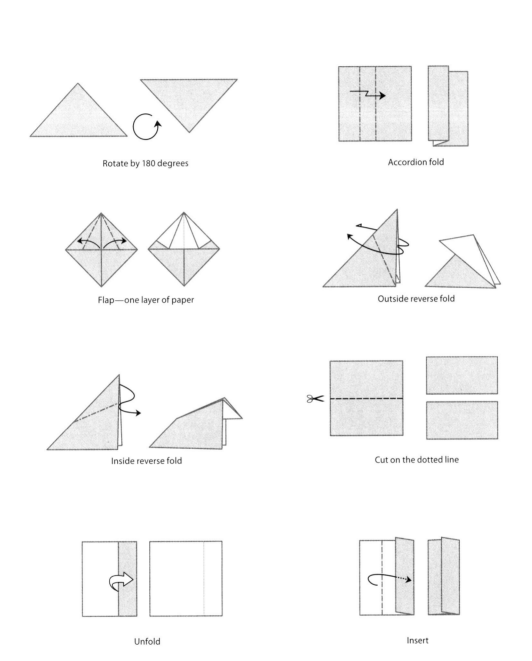

Rotate by 180 degrees

Accordion fold

Flap—one layer of paper

Outside reverse fold

Inside reverse fold

Cut on the dotted line

Unfold

Insert

Heart

A lovely heart for the romantic paper folder.

Earrings:
- 2 paper squares
  1" x 1" (3 x 3 cm)
- 2 earring posts
- Glue

Brooch:
- 1 paper square
  3" x 3" (7.5 x 7.5 cm)
- Brooch bar pin
- Glue

Bracelet:
- 5 paper squares
  1 1/4" x 1 1/4" (3.5 x 3.5 cm)
- 1 chain of 6 1/4" (16 cm)
- 6 jump rings
- 1 clasp

❶ Pre-crease in both directions.

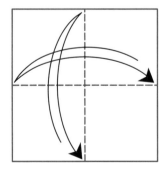

❷ Valley fold up to the center.

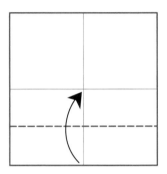

❸ Turn the paper over.

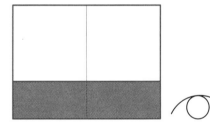

❹ Valley fold the corners to the center.

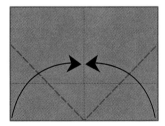

See page 9 for finishing a brooch, a ring, a hair accessory, or an earring post.

5 Turn the paper over.

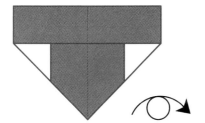

6 Valley fold the corners to the center.

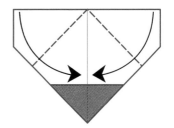

7 Valley fold the tip down, allowing the flap to pass under the white side pockets.

10 Turn the paper over.

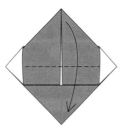

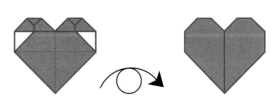

8 Valley fold the side corners.

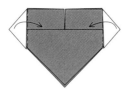

To create a bracelet, use a jump ring to make a hole in the finished heart models. Next, insert the ring through the hole and attach it to the chain. Finally, install a clasp (see page 8).

9 Valley fold the four corners down.

Iris

A pretty flower you can wear proudly to celebrate spring.

Earrings:
- 2 paper squares
  2" x 2" (5 x 5 cm)
- 2 earring hooks
- 2 jump rings

Brooch:
- 1 paper square
  3" x 3" (7.5 x 7.5 cm)
- 1 brooch bar pin
- Glue

Ring:
- 2 paper squares
  1 1/2" x 1 1/2" (4 x 4 cm)
- 1 finger ring with pad
- Glue

Necklace:
- 1 paper square
  4" x 4" (10 x 10 cm)
- 1 cord of 23 1/2" (60 cm)
- 3 beads
- 2 cord clamps
- 3 jump rings
- 1 clasp

❶ Pre-crease along the diagonals and turn over.

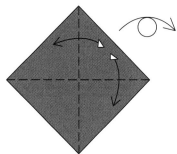

❷ Pre-crease the sides.

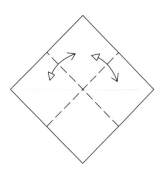

❸ Pre-crease the corners to the center.

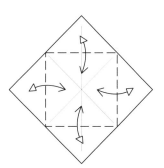

See page 10 for finishing an earring with a jump ring.

See page 9 for finishing a brooch.

To create this brooch, first make the leaf (see page 30), and glue that on the brooch bar pin pad. Then glue the iris on top.

19

4 Bring the corners up to meet.

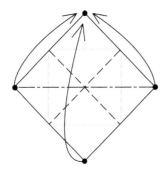

5 In progress . . .

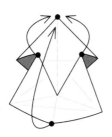

6 Spread apart the layers on the flap and squash it flat.

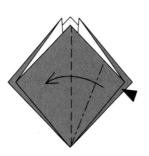

7 Pull the edge down, creasing the sides so they meet at the center.

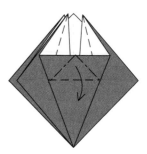

8 Valley fold the newly formed flap up.

9 Turn over.

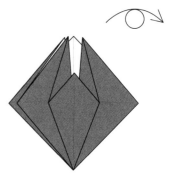

⑩ Repeat steps 6–8 on the indicated flap.

6-8

⑪ Fold over a short flap on each side.

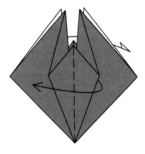

⑫ Repeat steps 6–8 on the front flap and on the rear flap.

6-8   6-8

See page 9 for finishing a ring.

⓭ Fold over a layer at each side.

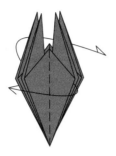

⓮ Valley fold the sides to the center. Repeat behind.

⓯ Swing over two layers at each side.

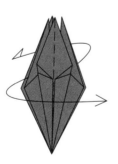

⓰ Valley fold the sides to the center. Repeat behind.

⓱ Fold the four petals outward, curling them slightly.

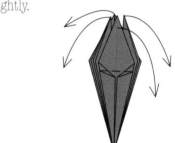

⓲ Completed Iris.

Pierce the bottom part of the model with a needle and attach a jump ring before introducing the cord in the link!

See page 11 for installing a cord clamp and page 8 for installing a clasp.

Rosette

An elaborate shape that will embellish your most sophisticated outfits!

Hair Accessories:
- 2 paper squares 2 1/4" x 2 1/4" (6 x 6 cm)
- 2 bobby pins with pads
- 2 pearls
- Patterned paper circles 1/2" (1.5 cm) in diameter
- Glue

Earrings:
- 2 paper squares 1 3/4" x 1 3/4" (4.5 x 4.5 cm)
- 2 earring hooks
- 2 earring hoops
- Nylon thread
- 2 crimp beads
- 2 sequins
- Glue

Brooch:
- 1 paper square 3" x 3" (7.5 x 7.5 cm)
- 1 paper square 1 1/2" x 1 1/2" (4 x 4 cm)
- 1 brooch bar pin
- 1 pearl
- Glue

Necklace:
- 1 paper square 3" x 3" (7.5 x 7.5 cm)
- 2 paper squares 2" x 2" (5 x 5 cm)
- 1 paper square 1 1/2" x 1 1/2" (4 x 4 cm)
- 1 ribbon 19 3/4" (50 cm)
- 3 sequins
- 2 ribbon clamps
- 2 jump rings
- 1 clasp
- Glue

1 Pre-crease along the diagonals.

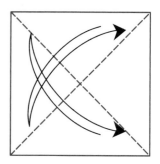

2 Valley fold the sides to the center.

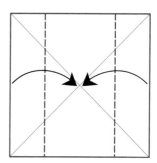

3 Pre-crease by folding the edges to the center and unfolding.

④ Pre-crease to the right.

⑤ Pre-crease to the left.

You can cut two circles from a patterned paper and glue them between your model and the pearl.

See page 9 for finishing a hair accessory.

6 Spread apart the lower corners and flatten.

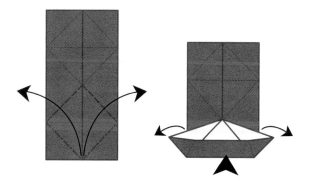

See page 9 for finishing a brooch and page 11 for installing a hoop.

7 Repeat this spread at the top.

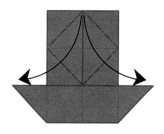

8 Valley fold one flap up and the opposite flap down.

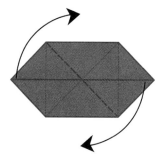

9 Spread apart the flaps and press them flat.

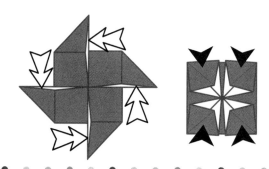

Glue a pearl
on the small piece,
and then glue the small
piece in the center of the
larger piece.

❿ Valley fold the flaps inward.

⓬ Mountain fold the four corners.

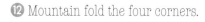

⓫ Open out a flap and squash it flat. Repeat this step on the 7 other flaps.

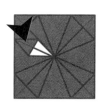

Glue a sequin in the center of the two smaller rosettes. To finish the large rosette, first glue a sequin in the center of the smaller rosette. Then, glue the smaller rosette onto the larger one.

See page 11 for installing a ribbon clamp and page 8 for installing a clasp.

Leaf

Add some greenery in your hair or behind your ear for the spring season!

Earrings:
- 2 paper squares
  1 1/2" x 1 1/2" (4 x 4 cm)
- 2 earring posts (with pad or hoop)
- 2 sequins
- Glue

Hair Accessories:
- 2 paper squares 3" x 3"
  (7.5 x 7.5 cm)
- 2 bobby pins with pads
- 6 sequins
- Glue

❷ Valley fold to the center.

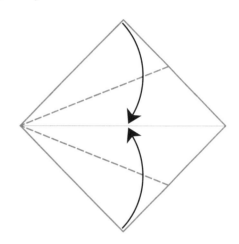

❶ Pre-crease along the diagonal.

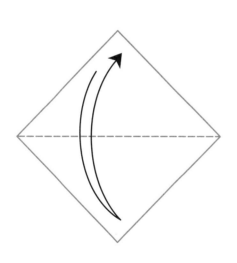

❸ Valley fold to the center.

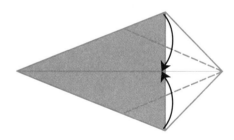

❹ Valley fold, so the opposite edges meet.

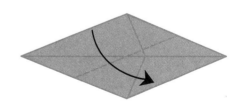

See page 9 for finishing a hair accessory or an earring post.

❺ Valley fold to the right.

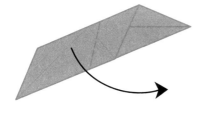

❻ Valley fold to the left.

You can add sequins to your hair accessories!

Box

Boxes can be jewels too!

Brooch:
- 3 paper squares
  3 1/4" x 3 1/4" (8 x 8 cm)
  (cover)
- 3 paper squares
  3" x 3" (7.7 x 7.7 cm) (bottom)
- 1 brooch bar pin
- Glue

Ring:
- 1 paper square
  1 1/4" x 1 1/4" (3.5 x 3.5 cm)
  (cover)
- 1 paper square
  1 1/4" x 1 1/4" (3.2 x 3.2 cm)
  (bottom)
- 1 finger ring with pad
- Glue

Bracelet:
- 6 paper squares
  2 1/4" x 2 1/4" (5.5 x 5.5 cm)
  (cover)
- 6 paper squares
  1 3/4" x 1 3/4" (4.7 x 4.7 cm)
  (bottom)
- 1 chain piece of 6 1/4"
  (16 cm)
- 6 screw eye pins
- 7 jump rings
- 1 clasp

❶ Pre-crease the sides in half.

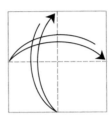

❷ Valley fold the four corners to the center and then rotate the paper by 90 degrees.

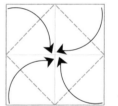

❸ Pre-crease the sides.

4 Open out the upper and lower flaps.

5 Valley fold the sides to the center.

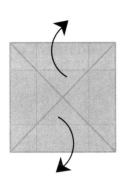

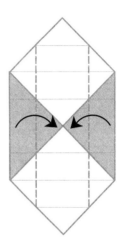

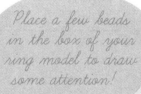

Place a few beads in the box of your ring model to draw some attention!

See page 9 for finishing a brooch and a ring.

6 Bring the three sides up to a 90-degree angle, adding the indicated folds.

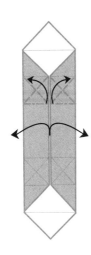

8 Repeat all the steps with the other paper to create the lid of the box.

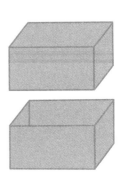

7 Bring the remaining sides up. Wrap the long flaps around the sides of the box, and press them flat into the bottom.

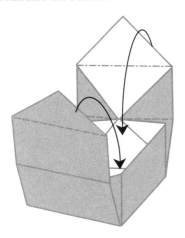

Attach each box to the chain with a jump ring.

See page 8 for installing a clasp and page 9 for installing a screw eye pin.

35

Butterfly

Perfect for a sunny day!

Bracelet:
- 1 paper square
  3" x 3" (7.5 x 7.5 cm)
- 1 ribbon of 6 1/4" (16 cm)
- 2 ribbon clamps
- 2 jump rings
- 1 clasp
- Glue

Hair Accessories:
- 2 paper squares
  1 1/4" x 1 1/4" (3.5 x 3.5 cm)
- 2 bobby pins with pads
- Glue

Earrings:
- 2 paper squares
  1 3/4" x 1 3/4" (4.5 x 4.5 cm)
- 2 earring posts
- 2 hoops
- Nylon thread
- 4 crimp beads

Ring:
- 1 paper square
  1 1/2" x 1 1/2" (4 x 4 cm)
- 1 finger ring with pad
- Glue

❶ Pre-crease the sides in half. Turn over.

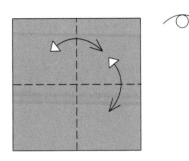

❷ Pre-crease along the diagonals.

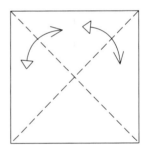

❸ Bring the bottom edge up to the top while pulling the sides inward.

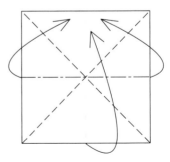

See page 11 for installing a ribbon clamp and page 8 for installing a clasp.

4 In progress . . . flatten completely.

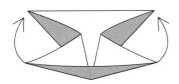

6 Turn over.

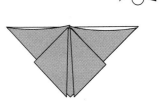

5 Valley fold the top flaps down.

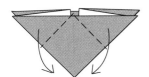

Glue your butterfly creation onto the middle of the bracelet.

7 Valley fold the flap a bit above the top edge. The hidden corners will squash flat while doing this.

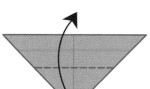

10 Mountain fold in half.

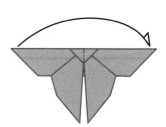

8 Flatten the sides and turn the paper over.

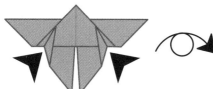

11 Fold the wings over at an angle and then spread the model open.

9 Valley fold the tip down.

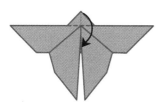

See page 9 for finishing a hair accessory, a ring, or an earring post.

See page 11
for finishing
a hoop.

Crane

The ideal bird for an origami piece of jewelry!

Earrings:
- 2 paper squares
  2" x 2" (5 x 5 cm)
- 2 earring hooks
- 2 pieces of chain 2" (5 cm)
- 2 screw eye pins
- 2 jump rings

Brooch:
- 1 paper square
  3" x 3" (7.5 x 7.5 cm)
- 1 brooch bar pin
- Glue

Hair Accessories:
- 2 paper squares
  2" x 2" (5 x 5 cm)
- 2 bobby pins with pads
- Glue

❷ Valley fold down.

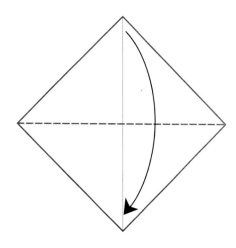

❸ Pre-crease the sides.

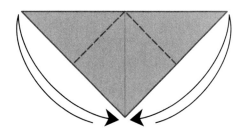

❶ Pre-crease along the diagonal.

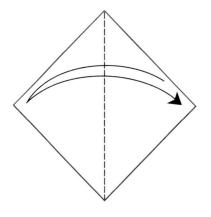

See page 9 for finishing a brooch.

4 Inside reverse fold the corners in and down and flatten them.

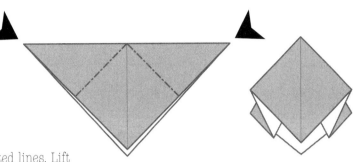

5 Pre-crease as shown by dotted lines. Lift the top flap up, allowing the sides to get pulled toward the center. Flatten and turn over the paper. Repeat this step on the other side.

6 Valley fold the sides to the center and turn the paper over. Repeat this step on the other side.

See page 10 for finishing an earring with a chain.

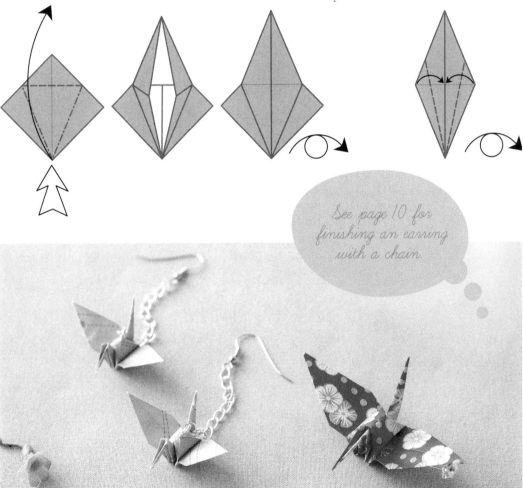

7 Fold over a layer at each side.

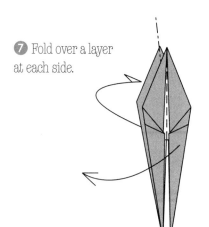

8 Valley fold the flaps to the top.

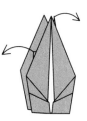

9 Valley fold the front flap down.

10 Fold over a layer at each side.

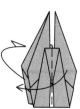

11 Slide the flaps in the center outward.

12 Slide the small flap out.

13 Open out the wings.

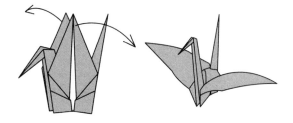

See page 9 for finishing a hair accessory.

Bow

Bracelet:
- 1 paper square
  4 3/4" x 4 3/4" (12 x 12 cm)
- 1 ribbon of 6 1/4" (16 cm)
- 1 pearl
- 2 ribbon clamps
- 2 jump rings
- 1 clasp

Ribbon Hair Accessories:
- 2 paper squares
  3" x 3" (7.5 x 7.5 cm)
- 2 bobby pins with pads
- 1 thin ribbon of 7 3/4" (20 cm)
- 4 round pearls
- Glue

Sequin Hair Accessories:
- 2 paper squares
  1 3/4" x 1 3/4" (4.5 x 4.5 cm)
- 2 bobby pins with pads
- 2 sequins
- Glue

Brooch:
- 1 paper square
  3 1/4" x 3 1/4" (8 x 8 cm)
- 1 paper square
  2 1/4" x 2 1/4" (6 x 6 cm)
- 1 brooch bar pin
- 1 sequin
- Glue

Earrings:
- 2 paper squares
  1 1/2" x 1 1/2" (4 x 4 cm)
- 2 earring posts
- 2 sequins
- Glue

❶ Pre-crease along the center.

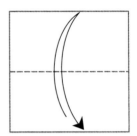

❷ Cut along the crease.

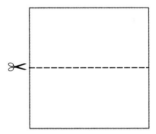

❸ Pre-crease along the center.

❹ Valley fold the corners to the center.

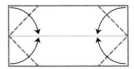

5 Valley fold the edges to the center.

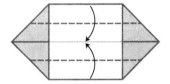

6 Valley fold in half and rotate the paper 90 degrees.

See page 11 for installing a ribbon clamp and page 8 for installing a clasp.

Glue a pearl onto the center of the piece!

7 Valley fold the top layer over while opening out the lower corner and pressing it flat.

8 Valley fold the flap back over.

9 Repeat steps 7–8 in mirror image.

7-8

10 Valley fold down the top corners, then turn the paper over.

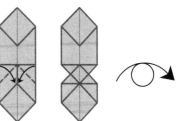

11 Valley fold down.

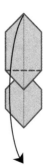

12 Valley fold the top corners to the center, then rotate the paper 90 degrees to the left.

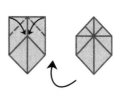

Cut two 4" (10 cm) pieces of ribbon. Insert the ends in a pearl, and make a knot to secure the pearl. Then, fold the ribbon and glue it on the pad of the bobby pin. Next, add a drop of glue to secure your origami bow on the bobby pin.

See page 9 for finishing a hair accessory.

13 Pull the top layer over, allowing the center to stretch apart flat.

14 Flatten the center, then turn the paper over.

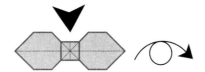

15 Valley fold in the outside corners.

16 Valley fold the four small inner corners, and then turn the paper over.

See page 9 for finishing a brooch and an earring.

Glue a sequin to the center of each model!

Star

Add some sparkle to your jewelry with stars!

Necklace:
- 10 paper rectangles 1/4" x 9 1/2" (0.7 x 24 cm)
- 1 paper rectangle 1/2" x 23 1/2" (1.5 x 60 cm)
- Nylon thread
- 2 cord clamps
- 2 jump rings
- 22 crimp beads
- 1 clasp

Brooch:
- 6 paper rectangles 1/2" x 11 3/4" (1 x 30 cm)
- 1 brooch bar pin
- Nylon thread
- 6 crimp beads
- 6 beads

Bracelet:
- 11 paper rectangles 1/2" x 11 3/4" (1 x 30 cm)
- Nylon thread
- 12 crimp beads
- 2 cord clamps
- 2 jump rings
- 1 clasp

Earring with pearls:
- 6 paper rectangles 1/4" x 9 1/2" (0.7 x 24 cm)
- 2 earring posts with hoops
- Nylon thread
- 8 crimp beads
- 2 beads

Earring with chain:
- 2 paper rectangles 1/2" x 11 3/4" (1 x 30 cm)
- 2 earring hoops
- 2 pieces of chain of 1 1/2" (4 cm)
- 2 screw eye pins
- 4 jump rings

❶ Form a knot at one end of the long and thin paper rectangle.

❷ Flatten.

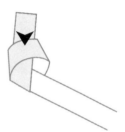

❸ Valley fold the protruding end inward.

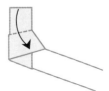

❹ Valley fold the longer side of the piece.

See page 9 for installing a crimp bead; page 11 for adding a cord clamp; and page 8 for finishing your necklace with a clasp.

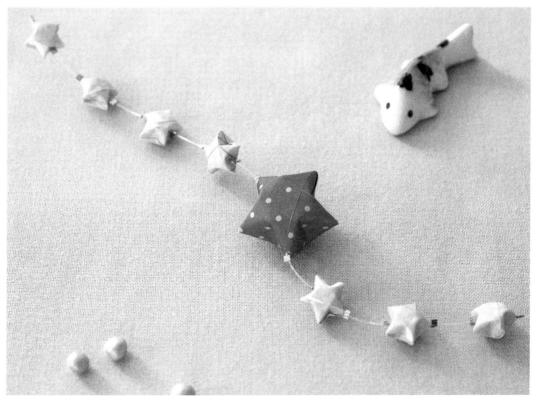

5 Mountain fold the long flap.

6 Continue wrapping the long flap around the remaining sides of the star.

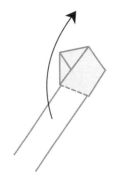

7 Keep on wrapping the long flap around. Insert the remaining end inside. If needed, cut off the excess paper.

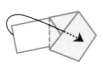

8 To give more volume to your star, pinch each side with your fingers.

See page 9 for installing a crimp bead; page 11 for adding a cord clamp; and page 8 for finishing your necklace with a clasp.

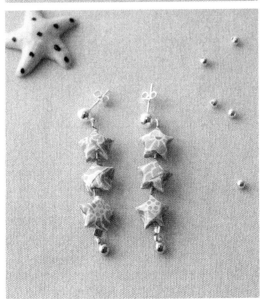

See page 10 for finishing an earring with a chain.

Menko

Make a fun geometrical present for your BFF!

Ring:
- 2 paper squares 2" x 2" (5 x 5 cm)
- 1 finger ring with pad
- Glue

Necklace:
- 2 paper squares 3" x 3" (7.5 x 7.5 cm)
- 6 paper squares
  1 1/2" x 1 1/2" (4 x 4 cm)
- 1 cord of 23 1/2" (60 cm)
- 3 chain pieces of 1" (2.5 cm)
- 9 jump rings
- 2 cord clamps
- 1 clasp

Brooch:
- 6 paper squares 3" x 3" (7.5 x 7.5 cm)
- 1 brooch bar pin
- Glue

Bracelet:
- 2 paper squares 3" x 3" (7.5 x 7.5 cm)
- 4 paper squares
  1 1/2" x 1 1/2" (4 x 4 cm)
- 2 pieces of cord of 3 1/4" (8 cm)
- 6 jump rings
- 2 cord clamps
- 1 clasp

Earrings with pearls:
- 4 paper squares
  1 1/2" x 1 1/2" (4 x 4 cm)
- 2 earring posts with pads
- Glue

❶ Valley fold down at 1/3 of your two paper squares.

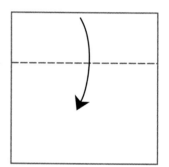

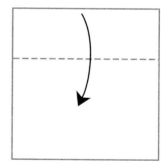

See page 9
for finishing
a ring.

② Valley fold up at 1/3 of your two paper squares.

③ Valley fold down the upper left corners of your two paper squares.

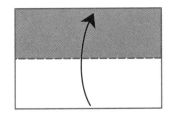

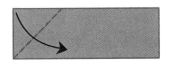

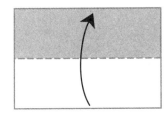

4 Valley fold up the lower right corner on both paper squares.

6 Place the first paper square in the center of the second paper square.

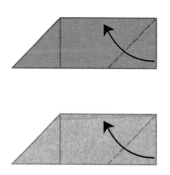

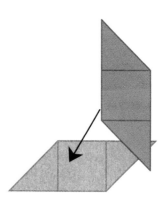

5 Rotate the first paper square left by 90 degrees.

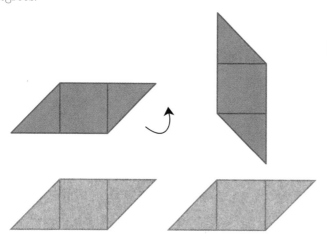

See page 11 for installing a cord clamp and page 8 for installing a clasp.

On the three smaller pieces, pierce one corner to insert a jump ring. Do the same on all corners of the larger creation. Then, attach the three smaller models to the larger one with a piece of chain.

7 Valley fold the right corner over.

9 Valley fold the left corner over.

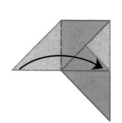

8 Valley fold the top corner down.

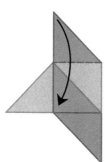

10 Tuck the remaining corner in the pocket.

See page 11 for installing a cord clamp and page 8 for installing a clasp.

See pages 8 & 9 for help in finishing these projects.

My Own Page

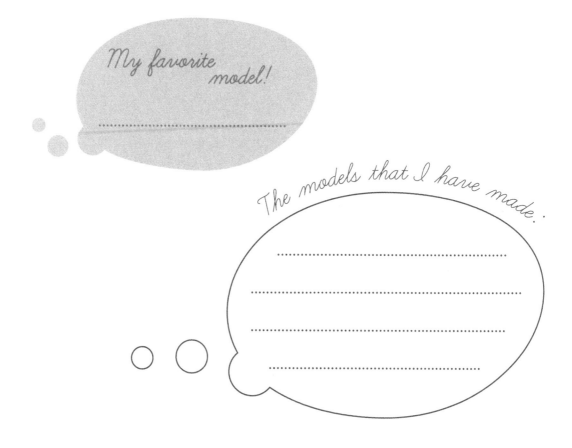

My favorite model!

....

The models that I have made:

....

....

....

....

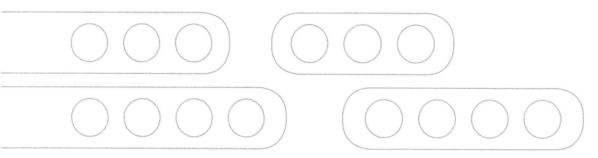

My own color arrangements:

The first model I created:

....

Models I have made for friends and family:

....

....

....

....

....

....